Night Snow

Also by Sally Nacker

Poems

Vireo

Night Snow

Sally Nacker

Kelsay Books

© 2017 Sally Nacker. All rights reserved. This material may not be reproduced in any form, published, reprinted, recorded, performed, broadcast, rewritten or redistributed without the explicit permission of Sally Nacker. All such actions are strictly prohibited by law.

Cover pastel and inside photolithograph by
Mary Lou Bierman, artist of various mediums including oil painting, drawing, pastel, pottery, book binding and printing.
Email: marialuisa2222@yahoo.com

ISBN: 13- 978-1-947465-24-4

Kelsay Books
Aldrich Press
www.kelsaybooks.com

For Grandmother Jenny, never forgotten
your red-winged blackbirds, your tulips

and for her daughter, my mother
I will always be with you

and for Laurie

Acknowledgments

The Fourth River (Tributaries): "Peony"
Grey Sparrow Journal, and its anthology *Snow Jewel*: "Winter Moment at a Vermont Inn"
Mezzo Cammin: An Online Journal of Formalist Poetry by Women: "Emily Dickinson's Amherst, Main Street," "Prayer During Rain," "Florist During During Loss," "During Stillness," "A Visit to Fort Juniper," "Left," "Winter Boughs," and "A Poem's in a Blade of Grass"
The Orchards: "Robin," "Night Snow"
The Red Wheel Barrow Literary Magazine, National Issue: "Study in White and Yellow"

"Ink Painting" was selected by Norwalk, Connecticut's Poet Laureate to ride the city bus, April, 2017

"Quieted" was written for the Fairfield University Art Museum's *ekphrasis v*, a poetry and prose reading in conjunction with the Michael Gallagher exhibit *Sketching the Landscape: A Plein Air Journal*—September, 2017

"Study in White and Yellow" was written, in part, to accompany musician/composer Jim Clark's jazz score "Spring at Last" during his concert *Old as New*—A Jazz and Poetry Collaboration at the Norwalk Public Library, April, 2017

Gratitude:

First and foremost, I wish to thank my husband, John (for always). Thanks to poet Leslie Schultz, my everlasting friend of the work and heart. Deepest thanks also to Dan Odegard, Baron Wormser, Henry Lyman, Kim Bridgford, Elizabeth Kirschner, Beth Clary, Vance Fazzino, Cynde Lahey, and Mary Read. Each of you have made a strong impression on me, and continue to enrich my life with your friendship. My world of poetry would not be so beautifully colored had you not entered it.

Thanks to Laurie and Greg, my dear sister and her husband. Thanks to Barbara and Lisa, my companions in flowers. Thanks to friends Alan and Michele, Mr. Bill and Joann, and Pat.

Finally, special thanks to author Michael C. White, along with Sonya Huber, and Elizabeth Hastings of the Fairfield University MFA Program in Creative Writing: your support endures, and must be acknowledged.

Contents

Ink Painting	13
Night Snow	14
Emily Dickinson's Amherst, Main Street	15
A Visit to Fort Juniper	16
Prayer During Rain	17
Florist During Loss	18
Winter Moment at a Vermont Inn	19
During Stillness	20
Sleeping House Cat	21
Left	22
Winter Boughs	23
Study in White and Yellow	24

Quieted	25
A Poem's in a Blade of Grass	26
The Binoculars	27
Recurring	28
Peony	29
Robin	30
About the Author	

Announced by all the trumpets of the sky / Arrives the snow…
—Ralph Waldo Emerson, "The Snow-Storm"

If I had never seen paintings and etchings of shadows on snow I think I should not have felt the beauty of footprints on my walk tonight.
—Robert Francis, *Travelling in Amherst*

The thing that makes me want to write is the same thing that makes me love that blade of grass. I can't separate them.
—W. S. Merwin, *PBS News Hour*

Ink Painting

Through a windowpane—
Old Japan in the fine
lines of pine branches.

Night Snow

for Robert Francis

The bird feeder hangs above night snow.
Below, footprints—shadowy, slow—
come and go. Only I know
the beauty of each moonlit hollow.
The prints are mine. It is song they follow.

Emily Dickinson's Amherst, Main Street

I stayed in a room at a B & B—
across from the old home of Emily—
where once stood her father's field of rye.
I heard the fall wind as I closed my eyes.

I slept in a house on the land she viewed
from her window overlooking the field—
her sherry eyes on the gold, swaying rye
tossing and glinting, and waving goodbye.

Goodbye to the rye, now gardens and homes,
goodbye to the rustling swish on the loam,
goodnight, goodnight, dear Emily, I said,
then dreamed of her asleep in her Homestead.

A Visit to Fort Juniper

> Amherst home of late poet, Robert Francis (1901-1987)

I sat inside his little house
all built out of hurricane pine.
Trees that had fallen in the gales
became his shelter, his design.

The house stands as the poet lived:
close to the ground, safe from high wind.
The house has windows on four sides
to view outside, and to view in.

I went to sense the solitude
the poet found there near the woods;
the solace and the quietude.
Sometimes he would not speak for days;

his sound was all within himself.
The poems found their way within,
the poems found their own way out.
A room for sleep, a small kitchen

is all he built, all he needed,
and one room warmed by a fire's glow.
Sitting in his small wood home, I
knew I was meant to come. I know.

Prayer During Rain

Grant me always the little birds.
They do not know me, or my words,

or how they lift me in the rain
with song that tenderly eases pain.

In a wet world like today, I know
their music during sorrow.

Rain tumbles from the gutter drain
onto the burying ground. Rain

shudders on the green leaves, then drips down.
Rain continues to come down.

Gift me hope when grief is long;
grant me a little floating song.

Florist During Loss

A heaven-blue, cotton gardener's glove
slips over the hand of my grief like love.

Through a mist of tears the yellow yarrow
softens, soothes my harrowed sorrow,

as do Asclepias for the butterfly, high swells
of sunflowers, purple Canterbury bells,

and delphiniums (fine tall stems of rich blue flowers—
little hanging bells of their own this hour).

Basho sang of the sound of the temple bell
coming out of the flowers. My flowers knell.

Come night, on my pillow I lay my head
as though in a ringing flowerbed.

Winter Moment at a Vermont Inn

Near a window, a silver spoon rests
on a saucer, beside a white teacup.
An old, oak rocking chair
is still. Winter's evening sun
touches each a little.

As the moon reflects the setting sun,
the objects glow, and deepen.
In dark, snow-quiet air,
I simply stare
at spoon, saucer, cup, and rocking chair.

During Stillness

There will be no table in heaven,
I would think,
or card upon it to send
or pen with ink.

No book with written word
or notebook with lines.
No embroidered bird,
or fork with tines,

will lie on my napkin
beside my plate.
No wine in
my cup when the night is late.

No window sill
to invite light, no window
at all. Perhaps no tree will
stand and sway tall. So

with mind and thoughts clear,
it is with joy that I sit
here. It is life I hold dear
in the ordinary quiet.

Sleeping House Cat

Winter morning—
you sleep in snow-lit,

quiet air. Black paws
tuck beneath you

on my bird-print, reading chair.
So still, the little birds

of azure and yellow dye.
Is song, alarm, or cry

ever heard
in their own white sky?

Left

In the narrow white boat
you took toward death—
through waters deep,
mysterious, and remote

to me—you seemed as though
you were asleep,
your face aglow
with your bright light

that began to dim in this land
as you moved to another
through the night.
Not there to hold your hand,

this is how I imagine it
must have been as you proved,
in the radiant, white room, the pure
holiness of your solitude.

Death is what mothers do alone;
daughters cannot come along
or pause the creaking boat. Your lantern shone
for you only.

Winter Boughs

In stillness I wake slow
to the slow return of sorrow.

I study from my window
white boughs drooping low.

A fluffed out little sparrow
sings in the icy glow.

Its song climbs with crescendo
up through the falling snow,

softens my grief, opens, allows,
wakes me to beauty in the boughs.

Study in White and Yellow

I.

Icicles. Snow. Sheen
of moonglow. Frost bitten pane.
The heart's high-pitched heat.
Wailing. Lament. Freezing rain.

North Star in a vast, icy sky.
Hospital. A face at death.
Holiness. Snow blast.
Sharp cry. My own breath.

II.

Forsythia. Buttercup. Sassafras.
Swallowtail butterfly. Dandelion. Daffodil.
Singing finches in new golden coats.
Trout lily. Nest. Jonquil.

Honey. Bamboo. Hope.
Rain slicker. Bright sun. Waking up.
Canary Bird cascading rose.
Upright yellow tulip cup.

Quieted

> An apology to artist Michael Gallagher, whose *Sketching the Landscape: A Plein Air Journal* is on exhibit at the Fairfield University Art Museum, 2017

Here, on a late spring day—
birdsong shut out by museum walls—
in silence, in stillness, I study
Maine, your wintry landscape
white as unfolding white peony,
but cold as clouds. I have not been able to write
the poem I promised you.

My own art, so lively last winter,
has gone quiet, the life drawn
out of it. Perhaps, in a roomful of framed seasons,
this is what draws
me to your snow: the memory of the beauty
I once wrote in, and about; your penciled trees
offering their vast, brown shadows

to the snow while day drips into night,
never regretful. The sanctity of snow graces the mountaintop
you have placed in the background like Mount Fuji.
How am I deserving of poetry, the heaven it offers,
the authenticity it reveals
when I feel lost and untrue? The beauty?
Bless your white air. I miss the snow.

A Poem's in a Blade of Grass

A poem's in a blade of grass.
As a little girl, this I found
before I knew I knew the grass

or how a poem comes to pass.
I heard a quiet, whistling sound
of poems in the blades of grass.

I came to learn my own compass
by sound around me on the ground.
I knew, I knew, I knew the grass,

the green blades, the widening mass
of hymns, or prayers, on every mound.
A poem's in a blade of grass.

I turn my ear to nature's Mass,
recalling how the subtle sound—
before I knew I knew the grass—

awoke me to a holiness,
before I wrote the sound I found
in poems in the blades of grass,
before I knew I knew the grass.

The Binoculars

for my husband

While you walk in the woods
today, I sit quietly
at home, listening
to birds chatter
through our open window.

Gazing out the window,
I think how each time I lift
the binoculars you gave me as a birthday
gift, my grieving world clears,
and life becomes fresh,
and beautiful in color.

At Hammonasset, you recall, the lenses
brought into crisp view
a secretive saltmarsh sparrow on a fence post, whose
orange markings I felt exhilarated on identifying
with my Sibley guide,
and my new eyes.

Today, my binoculars rest,
and I recline with inward eye,
and listen, imagining your breath,
your footsteps in metered measure on a path,
birdsong on either side.

Recurring

for my mother, 1933-2012

In my dream, I carry you
over the green hill
of heaven— it is a green
hill, and I see it as heaven—
and I carry you, and I carry you,
and that is all there is.
The day is clear, night comes.
The night is clear.
I am never tired.
I am ever holy in heart.

Peony

for B.W.

You bring home a peony bush
to plant with your dog's ashes.
Too late for medicine, or hope,
but not for beauty. Each June,
an effusion of vivid blossoms
will open, blessing air. And all month,
you will bless your beloved friend
in open prayer. July will wander
cruelly in, like death again, each year.
New life will follow each next spring
as fresh buds loosen and declare.

Robin

When you first see spring, announce it clearly:
cheerily, cheery, cheerily.
Keep your flight note high, and trilled.
Hop. Sing with a will.

Let your orange heart shine. April
rains will loosen the earth for you, thrill
you with sweet worms. Seek open ground,
green lawn, insect sound.

That said, safe blessedness of home is best.
Seek a private tree for your own nest.
Build. Gather grasses, mud, and hair—
quietly. Take care.

About the Author

After receiving recognition as finalist (Fairfield Book Prize), semifinalist (Crab Orchard Series in Poetry), and honorable mention (Homebound Publications), Sally's first book, *Vireo*, was published by Kelsay Books in 2015. Shortly afterwards, Dr. Kim Bridgford invited her to be a featured poet at *Poetry by the Sea: A Global Conference* in Madison, CT. Sally earned her MFA in Poetry from Fairfield University in 2013. She resides in New England with her husband, and their two cats, and works in flowers. She invites you to visit her website at www.sallynacker.com.

www.ingramcontent.com/pod-product-compliance
Lightning Source LLC
LaVergne TN
LVHW021627080426
835510LV00019B/2786